Draw a line to connect each shape to the correct name.

circle

rectangle

triangle

square

rhombus

Circle the set of bugs in each row that is greatest. Draw an X on the set of bugs in each row that is least.

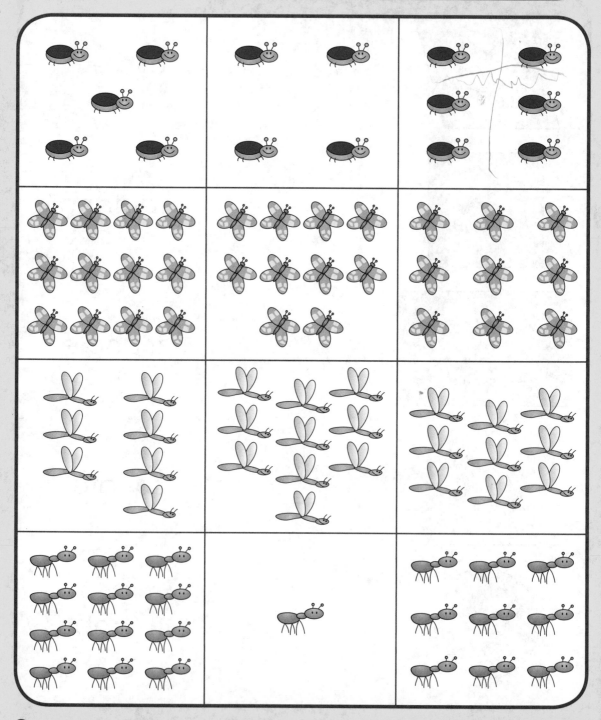

CD-104359   © Carson-Dellosa

Solve each problem.

1. $\begin{array}{r} 1 \\ +5 \\ \hline 6 \end{array}$

2. $\begin{array}{r} 2 \\ +0 \\ \hline 5 \end{array}$

3. $\begin{array}{r} 3 \\ +1 \\ \hline \end{array}$

4. $\begin{array}{r} 0 \\ +1 \\ \hline \end{array}$

5. $\begin{array}{r} 3 \\ +2 \\ \hline 0 \end{array}$

6. $\begin{array}{r} 1 \\ +2 \\ \hline \end{array}$

7. $\begin{array}{r} 6 \\ +0 \\ \hline \end{array}$

8. $\begin{array}{r} 2 \\ +2 \\ \hline \end{array}$

9. $\begin{array}{r} 4 \\ +0 \\ \hline \end{array}$

10. $\begin{array}{r} 2 \\ +3 \\ \hline \end{array}$

11. $\begin{array}{r} 1 \\ +1 \\ \hline \end{array}$

12. $\begin{array}{r} 0 \\ +0 \\ \hline \end{array}$

13. $\begin{array}{r} 1 \\ +0 \\ \hline \end{array}$

14. $\begin{array}{r} 2 \\ +1 \\ \hline \end{array}$

15. $\begin{array}{r} 1 \\ +3 \\ \hline \end{array}$

Color the circles purple. Color the triangles red. Color the rectangles green. Color the squares orange.

CD-104359

Solve each problem.

1.   5
   + 4
   ———
     9

2.   7
   + 0
   ———

3.   6
   + 1
   ———

4.   3
   + 3
   ———

5.   3
   + 6
   ———

6.   4
   + 4
   ———

7.   2
   + 7
   ———

8.   0
   + 6
   ———

9.   5
   + 3
   ———

CD-104359

Write letters to describe each pattern. The first one has been done for you.

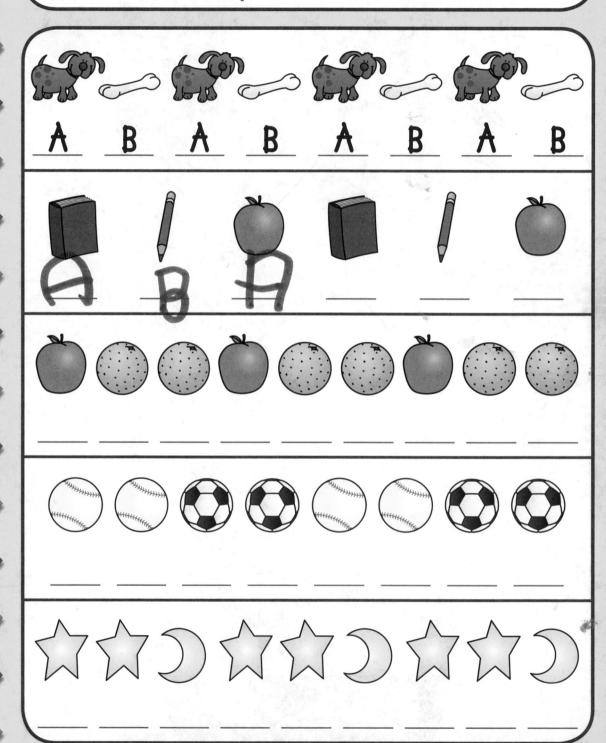

A B A B A B A B

A B A ___ ___ ___

___ ___ ___ ___ ___ ___ ___ ___ ___

___ ___ ___ ___ ___ ___ ___ ___

___ ___ ___ ___ ___ ___ ___ ___

CD-104359

Solve each problem.

1. $\begin{array}{r} 8 \\ -3 \\ \hline 6 \end{array}$

2. $\begin{array}{r} 7 \\ +5 \\ \hline 2 \end{array}$

3. $\begin{array}{r} 9 \\ -1 \\ \hline 8 \end{array}$

4. $\begin{array}{r} 8 \\ -0 \\ \hline 8 \end{array}$

5. $\begin{array}{r} 6 \\ -3 \\ \hline \end{array}$

6. $\begin{array}{r} 5 \\ -1 \\ \hline \end{array}$

7. $\begin{array}{r} 6 \\ -2 \\ \hline \end{array}$

8. $\begin{array}{r} 4 \\ -0 \\ \hline \end{array}$

9. $\begin{array}{r} 9 \\ -6 \\ \hline \end{array}$

10. $\begin{array}{r} 8 \\ -5 \\ \hline \end{array}$

11. $\begin{array}{r} 7 \\ -4 \\ \hline \end{array}$

12. $\begin{array}{r} 5 \\ -3 \\ \hline \end{array}$

13. $\begin{array}{r} 9 \\ -8 \\ \hline \end{array}$

14. $\begin{array}{r} 7 \\ -6 \\ \hline \end{array}$

15. $\begin{array}{r} 8 \\ -2 \\ \hline \end{array}$

CD-104359

Draw a picture using 2 triangles, 3 squares, 5 circles, and 6 rectangles.

☐ square ▭ rectangle △ triangle ○ circle

CD-104359

Solve each problem.

1. $\begin{array}{r} 7 \\ +2 \\ \hline \end{array}$ 2. $\begin{array}{r} 9 \\ +1 \\ \hline \end{array}$ 3. $\begin{array}{r} 5 \\ -3 \\ \hline \end{array}$

4. $\begin{array}{r} 8 \\ +1 \\ \hline \end{array}$ 5. $\begin{array}{r} 10 \\ +0 \\ \hline \end{array}$ 6. $\begin{array}{r} 9 \\ -3 \\ \hline \end{array}$

7. $\begin{array}{r} 5 \\ -2 \\ \hline \end{array}$ 8. $\begin{array}{r} 10 \\ -2 \\ \hline \end{array}$ 9. $\begin{array}{r} 7 \\ +0 \\ \hline \end{array}$

10. $\begin{array}{r} 7 \\ +1 \\ \hline \end{array}$ 11. $\begin{array}{r} 9 \\ -6 \\ \hline \end{array}$ 12. $\begin{array}{r} 2 \\ +2 \\ \hline \end{array}$

13. $\begin{array}{r} 8 \\ -3 \\ \hline \end{array}$ 14. $\begin{array}{r} 6 \\ +2 \\ \hline \end{array}$ 15. $\begin{array}{r} 7 \\ -5 \\ \hline \end{array}$

1.

_____ tens _____ ones

_____ total

2.

_____ ten _____ ones

_____ total

3.

_____ tens _____ ones

_____ total

4.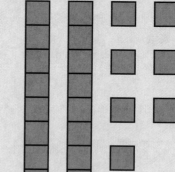

_____ tens _____ ones

_____ total

Solve each problem.

1.
$$\begin{array}{r} 8 \\ -\ 1 \\ \hline \end{array}$$

2.
$$\begin{array}{r} 8 \\ +\ 2 \\ \hline \end{array}$$

3.
$$\begin{array}{r} 5 \\ -\ 2 \\ \hline \end{array}$$

4.
$$\begin{array}{r} 9 \\ -\ 5 \\ \hline \end{array}$$

5.
$$\begin{array}{r} 9 \\ +\ 0 \\ \hline \end{array}$$

6.
$$\begin{array}{r} 6 \\ -\ 2 \\ \hline \end{array}$$

7.
$$\begin{array}{r} 5 \\ -\ 3 \\ \hline \end{array}$$

8.
$$\begin{array}{r} 8 \\ -\ 3 \\ \hline \end{array}$$

9.
$$\begin{array}{r} 7 \\ +\ 1 \\ \hline \end{array}$$

10.
$$\begin{array}{r} 8 \\ +\ 1 \\ \hline \end{array}$$

11.
$$\begin{array}{r} 9 \\ -\ 6 \\ \hline \end{array}$$

12.
$$\begin{array}{r} 4 \\ +\ 2 \\ \hline \end{array}$$

13.
$$\begin{array}{r} 8 \\ -\ 2 \\ \hline \end{array}$$

14.
$$\begin{array}{r} 3 \\ -\ 2 \\ \hline \end{array}$$

15.
$$\begin{array}{r} 9 \\ +\ 1 \\ \hline \end{array}$$

Write how many tens and ones. Write the total.

1.

_____ tens _____ ones

_____ total

2.

_____ tens _____ ones

_____ total

3.

_____ tens _____ ones

_____ total

4.

_____ tens _____ ones

_____ total

CD-104359

Draw and color the shape that comes next in each pattern.

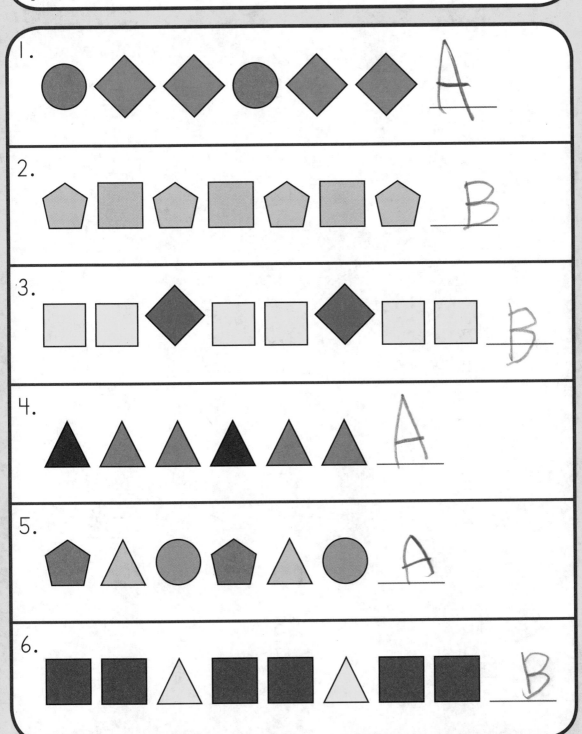

1. A

2. B

3. B

4. A

5. A

6. B

 CD-104359

Solve each problem.

1. $\begin{array}{r} 14 \\ -\ 2 \\ \hline \end{array}$
2. $\begin{array}{r} 12 \\ -\ 2 \\ \hline \end{array}$
3. $\begin{array}{r} 17 \\ -\ 8 \\ \hline \end{array}$

4. $\begin{array}{r} 18 \\ -\ 8 \\ \hline \end{array}$
5. $\begin{array}{r} 18 \\ -\ 1 \\ \hline \end{array}$
6. $\begin{array}{r} 10 \\ -\ 3 \\ \hline \end{array}$

7. $\begin{array}{r} 17 \\ -\ 4 \\ \hline \end{array}$
8. $\begin{array}{r} 16 \\ -\ 4 \\ \hline \end{array}$
9. $\begin{array}{r} 14 \\ -\ 3 \\ \hline \end{array}$

10. $\begin{array}{r} 18 \\ -\ 2 \\ \hline \end{array}$
11. $\begin{array}{r} 17 \\ -\ 6 \\ \hline \end{array}$
12. $\begin{array}{r} 15 \\ -\ 6 \\ \hline \end{array}$

13. $\begin{array}{r} 16 \\ -\ 2 \\ \hline \end{array}$
14. $\begin{array}{r} 15 \\ -\ 7 \\ \hline \end{array}$
15. $\begin{array}{r} 16 \\ -\ 5 \\ \hline \end{array}$

CD-104359

Look at the pictures in each box. Circle the comparison that is true.

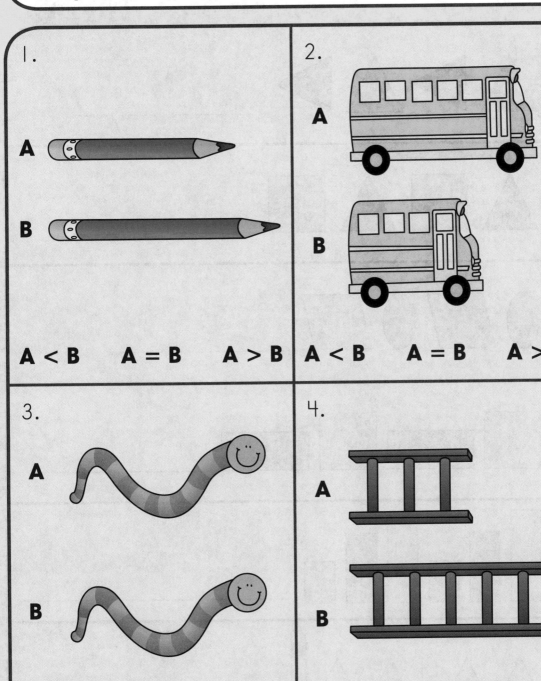

1.

A

B

A < B   A = B   A > B

2.

A

B

A < B   A = B   A > B

3.

A

B

A < B   A = B   A > B

4.

A

B

A < B   A = B   A > B

Draw and color the shapes that come next in each pattern.

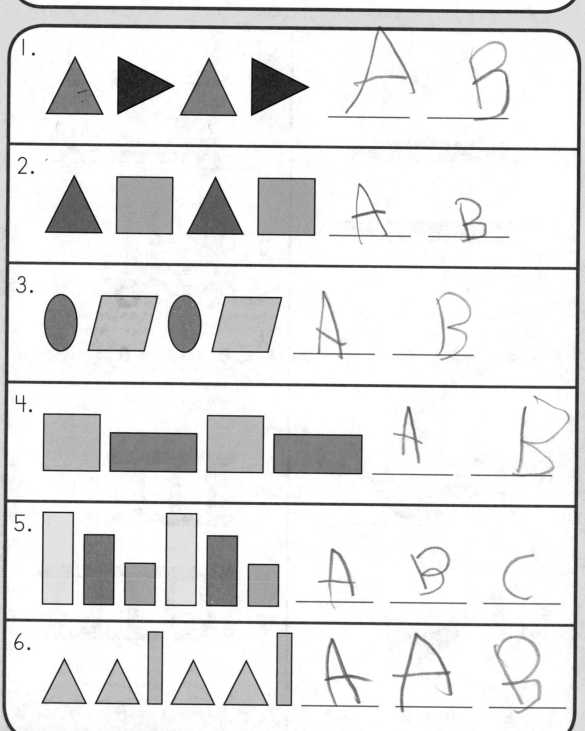

1.

2.

3.

4.

5.

6.

 CD-104359

Write the fraction for each colored part.

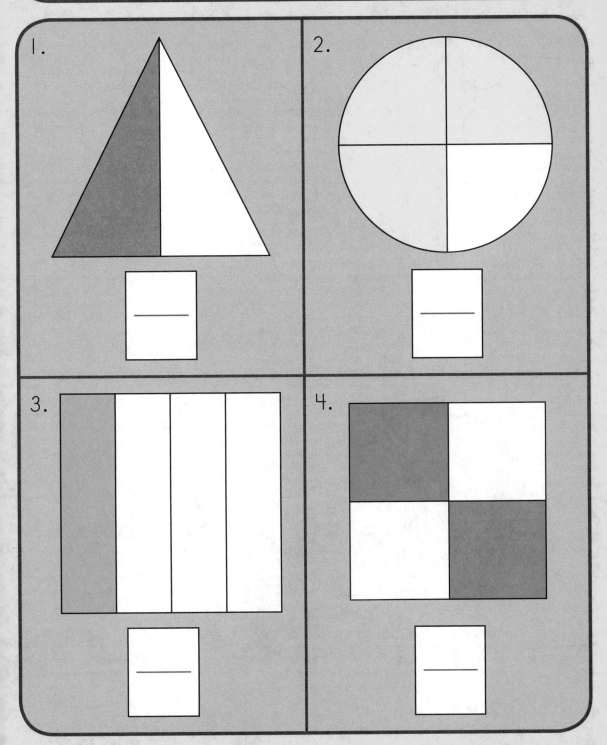

1.

2.

3.

4.

Write > or < to compare each pair of numbers.

1. 11 ◯ 13   2. 18 ◯ 47   3. 62 ◯ 56

4. 21 ◯ 14   5. 73 ◯ 85   6. 75 ◯ 33

7. 39 ◯ 27   8. 55 ◯ 75   9. 44 ◯ 50

10. 62 ◯ 54   11. 21 ◯ 16   12. 38 ◯ 83

CD-104359

Color $\frac{1}{3}$ of each shape.

1.

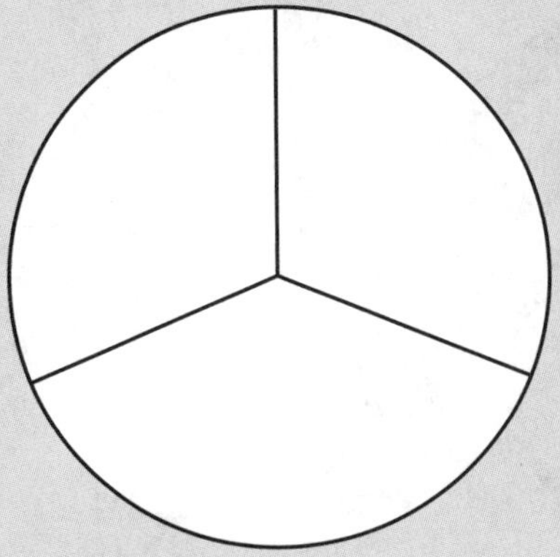

2.

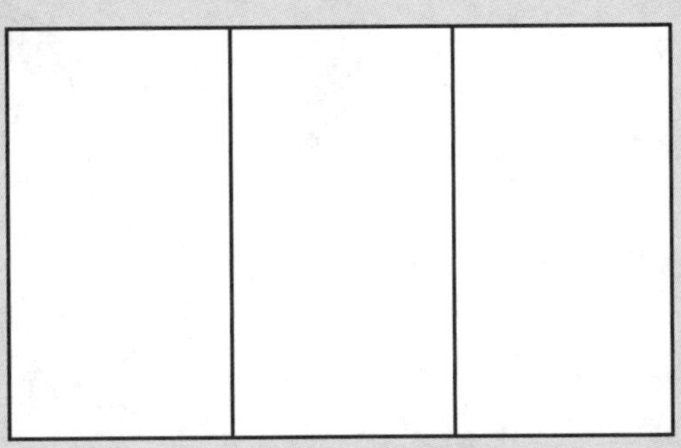

3.

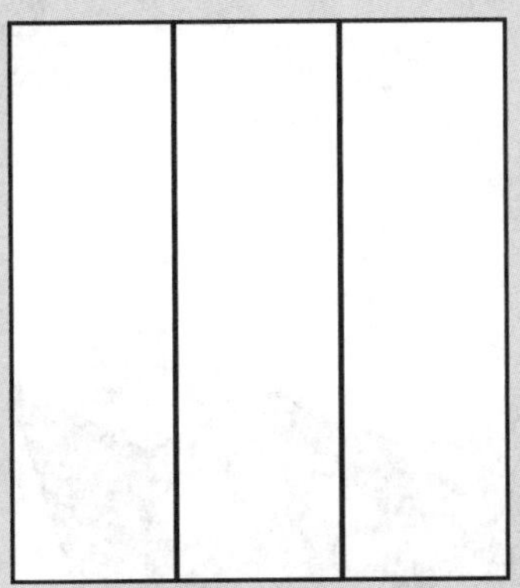

4.

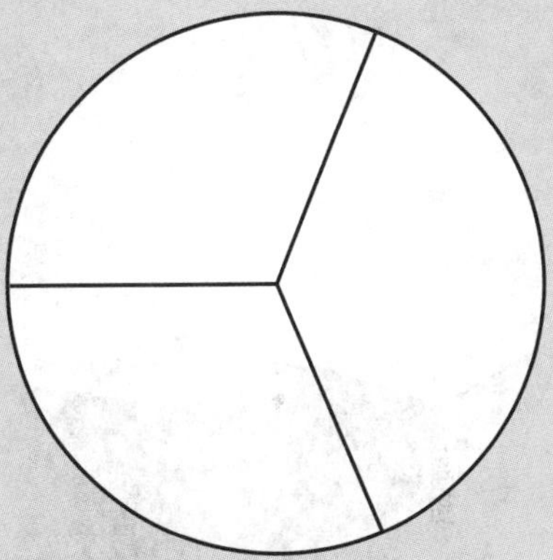

5.

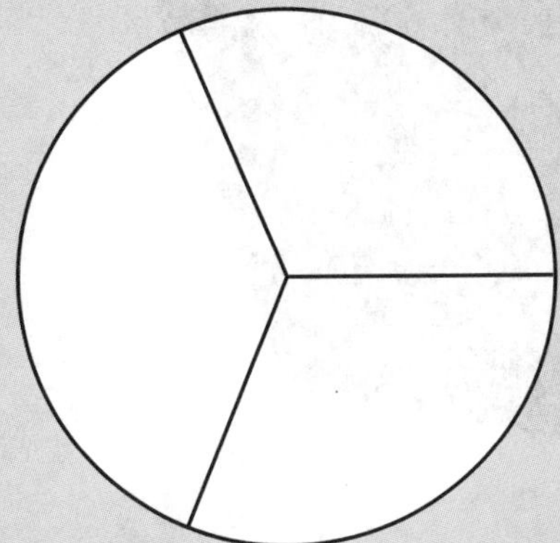

6.

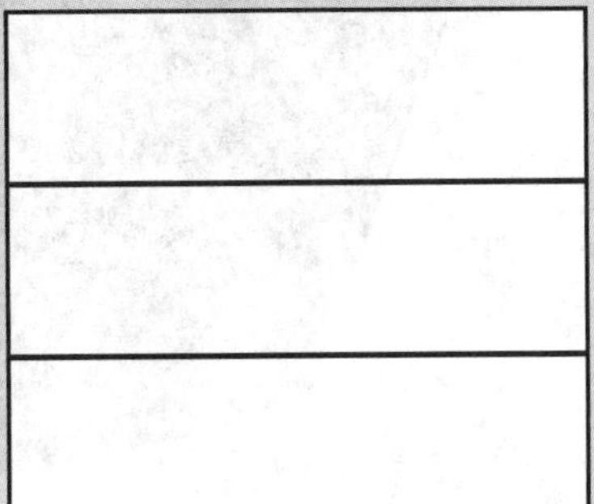

Connect the dots from 2 to 30. Count by 2s. Start at the ★.

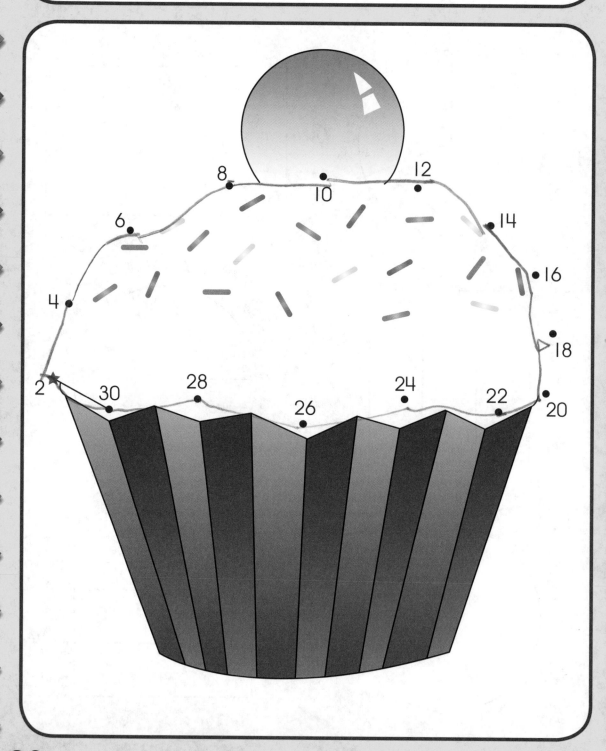

CD-104359 © Carson-Dellosa

Solve each problem.

1. $\begin{array}{r} 1 \\ + 8 \\ \hline \end{array}$

2. $\begin{array}{r} 15 \\ + 3 \\ \hline \end{array}$

3. $\begin{array}{r} 10 \\ + 8 \\ \hline \end{array}$

4. $\begin{array}{r} 12 \\ + 4 \\ \hline \end{array}$

5. $\begin{array}{r} 8 \\ + 9 \\ \hline \end{array}$

6. $\begin{array}{r} 9 \\ + 3 \\ \hline \end{array}$

7. $\begin{array}{r} 11 \\ + 2 \\ \hline \end{array}$

8. $\begin{array}{r} 11 \\ + 7 \\ \hline \end{array}$

9. $\begin{array}{r} 12 \\ + 5 \\ \hline \end{array}$

10. $\begin{array}{r} 8 \\ + 2 \\ \hline \end{array}$

11. $\begin{array}{r} 8 \\ + 5 \\ \hline \end{array}$

12. $\begin{array}{r} 9 \\ + 9 \\ \hline \end{array}$

13. $\begin{array}{r} 7 \\ + 6 \\ \hline \end{array}$

14. $\begin{array}{r} 9 \\ + 7 \\ \hline \end{array}$

15. $\begin{array}{r} 13 \\ + 5 \\ \hline \end{array}$

Count the money in each row. Write the total value.

1. (5¢) (5¢) (5¢) (5¢) (5¢)
   (5¢) (5¢) (5¢) (5¢)
   _____ ¢

2. (5¢) (5¢) (5¢) (5¢) (5¢) (5¢)
   (5¢) (5¢) (5¢) (5¢) (5¢)
   _____ ¢

3. (5¢) (5¢) (5¢) (5¢) (5¢) (5¢)
   (5¢) (5¢) (5¢) (5¢) (5¢) (5¢)
   _____ ¢

4. (10¢) (10¢) (10¢) (10¢)
   _____ ¢

5. (10¢) (10¢) (10¢) (10¢) (10¢) (10¢)
   _____ ¢

6. (10¢) (10¢) (10¢) (10¢) (10¢) (10¢) (10¢)
   _____ ¢

CD-104359

Solve each problem.

1.
```
    5
    3
  + 4
  ___
```

2.
```
   10
    0
  + 5
  ___
```

3.
```
    7
    2
  + 8
  ___
```

4.
```
    4
    5
  + 2
  ___
```

5.
```
    2
    3
  + 9
  ___
```

6.
```
    8
    6
  + 2
  ___
```

7.
```
    4
    5
  + 7
  ___
```

8.
```
    6
    2
  + 6
  ___
```

9.
```
    3
    7
  + 5
  ___
```

10.
```
    4
    2
  + 8
  ___
```

11.
```
    1
    1
  + 5
  ___
```

12.
```
    4
    0
  + 6
  ___
```

CD-104359

Use the graph to answer each question.

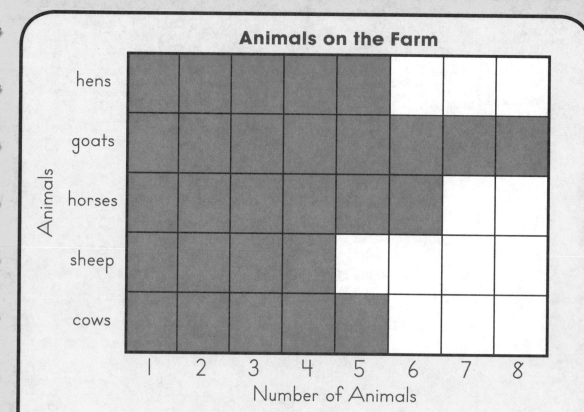

Animals on the Farm

Animals

hens
goats
horses
sheep
cows

Number of Animals

1. How many cows are on the farm? _____

2. How many goats are on the farm? _____

3. There are 6 _____ on the farm.

4. There are 4 _____ on the farm.

5. There are 5 _____ and _____

on the farm.

CD-104359

Use a ruler to find each object's length in inches. Measure the line below the object.

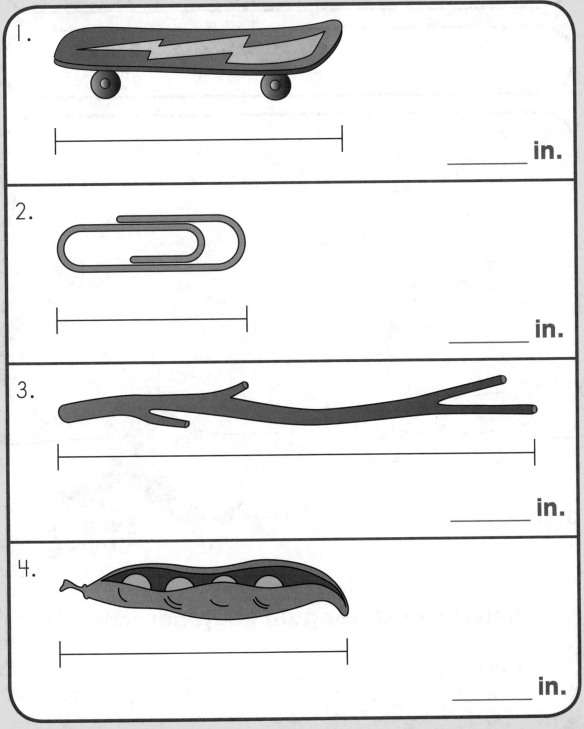

1. _____ in.

2. _____ in.

3. _____ in.

4. _____ in.

Solve each problem. Match the answers to the letters in the key. To solve the riddle, write the letters in order on the lines.

2 = **N**	4 = **W**	6 = **A**	7 = **K**
9 = **O**	10 = **B**	14 = **S**	15 = **N**

1. $9 + 5 =$ _____

2. $13 + 2 =$ _____

3. $12 - 3 =$ _____

4. $15 - 11 =$ _____

5. $6 + 4 =$ _____

6. $5 + 1 =$ _____

7. $15 - 13 =$ _____

8. $15 - 8 =$ _____

Where does a penguin keep her money?

In a ___ ___ ___ ___ ___ ___ ___ ___

26   CD-104359   © Carson-Dellosa

Connect the dots from 5 to 50. Count by 5s.
Start at the ★. Color the picture.

Solve each problem. Match the answers to the letters in the key. To solve the riddle, write the letters in order on the lines.

1 = **I**	2 = **G**	3 = **H**	4 = **E**	5 = **B**
6 = **R**	7 = **N**	8 = **O**	9 = **D**	

1. 8 – 1 = _____

2. 9 – 5 = _____

3. 5 – 4 = _____

4. 5 – 3 = _____

5. 2 + 1 = _____

6. 7 – 2 = _____

7. 4 + 4 = _____

8. 5 + 1 = _____

9. 7 – 4 = _____

10. 9 – 1 = _____

11. 6 + 2 = _____

12. 3 + 6 = _____

Where do horses live?
In a

" ___ ___ ___ ___ – ___ ___ ___ ___ ___ ___ "

CD-104359

Count the money in each jar. Write the total value.

1.

_____ ¢

2.

_____ ¢

3.

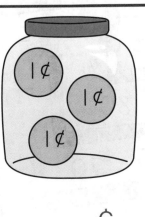

_____ ¢

4.

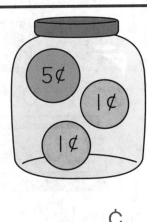

_____ ¢

5.

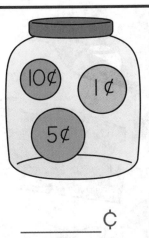

_____ ¢

6.

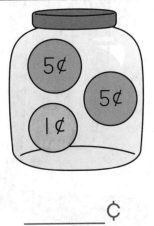

_____ ¢

CD-104359

Count by 10s. Draw a line through the maze from 10 to 200 to help the mouse find the cheese.

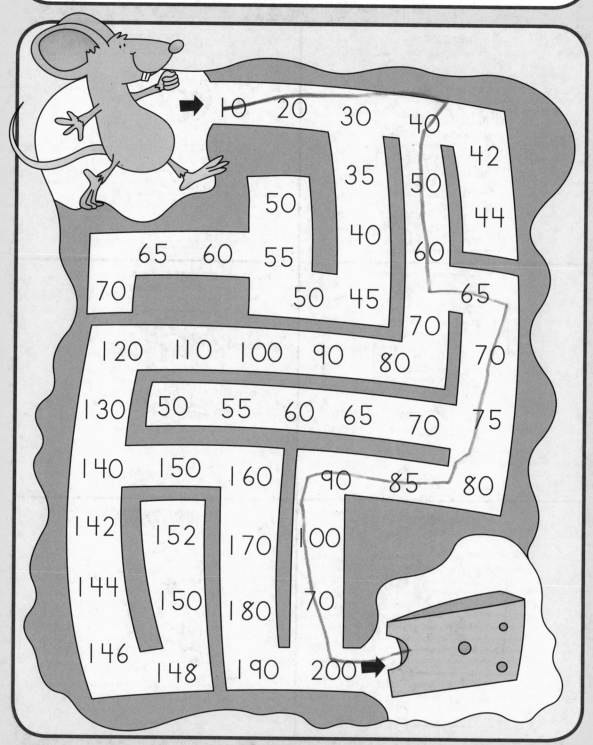

CD-104359 © Carson-Dellosa

Page 1

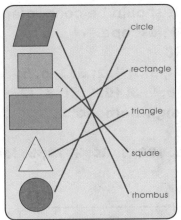

Page 2

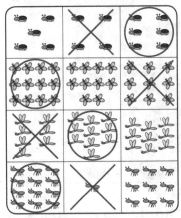

Page 3

1. 6; 2. 2; 3. 4; 4. 1; 5. 5; 6. 3;
7. 6; 8. 4; 9. 4; 10. 5; 11. 2; 12. 0;
13. 1; 14. 3; 15. 4

Page 4

Page 5

1. 9; 2. 7; 3. 7; 4. 6; 5. 9; 6. 8;
7. 9; 8. 6; 9. 8

Page 6

Row 2: ABCABC; Row 3: ABBABB;
Row 4: AABBAABB; Row 5: AABAAB

Page 7

1. 5; 2. 2; 3. 8; 4. 8; 5. 3; 6. 4;
7. 4; 8. 4; 9. 3; 10. 3; 11. 3; 12. 2;
13. 1; 14. 1; 15. 6

Page 8

Drawings will vary.

Page 9

1. 9; 2. 10; 3. 2; 4. 9; 5. 10; 6. 6;
7. 3; 8. 8; 9. 7; 10. 8; 11. 3; 12. 4;
13. 5; 14. 8; 15. 2

Page 10

1. 2 tens, 4 ones, 24 total;
2. 1 ten, 5 ones, 15 total;
3. 3 tens, 6 ones, 36 total;
4. 2 tens, 7 ones, 27 total

Page 11

1. 7; 2. 10; 3. 3; 4. 4; 5. 9; 6. 4;
7. 2; 8. 5; 9. 8; 10. 9; 11. 3; 12. 6;
13. 6; 14. 1; 15. 10

Page 12

1. 3 tens, 4 ones, 34 total;
2. 4 tens, 5 ones, 45 total;
3. 4 tens, 9 ones, 49 total;
4. 2 tens, 8 ones, 28 total

Page 13

1. ⬤; 2. ◻; 3. ◆; 4. ▲; 5. ⬠; 6. △

Page 14

1. 12; 2. 10; 3. 9; 4. 10; 5. 17;
6. 7; 7. 13; 8. 12; 9. 11; 10. 16;
11. 11; 12. 9; 13. 14; 14. 8; 15. 11

Page 15

1. A < B; 2. A > B; 3. A = B; 4. A < B

A

Page 16
1. △ ▶; 2. △ ▮; 3. ⬭ ▱;
4. ▮ ▬; 5. ▯ ▮ ▮; 6. △ △ ▮

Page 17
1. $\frac{1}{2}$; 2. $\frac{3}{4}$; 3. $\frac{1}{4}$; 4. $\frac{2}{4}$ or $\frac{1}{2}$

Page 18
1. <; 2. <; 3. >; 4. >; 5. <; 6. >; 7. >;
8. <; 9. <; 10. >; 11. >; 12. <

Page 19
Answers will vary but one space in each shape should be colored.

Page 20
The dots should be connected to form a cupcake.

Page 21
1. 9; 2. 18; 3. 18; 4. 16; 5. 17;
6. 12; 7. 13; 8. 18; 9. 17; 10. 10;
11. 13; 12. 18; 13. 13; 14. 16;
15. 18

Page 22
1. 45¢; 2. 55¢; 3. 60¢; 4. 40¢;
5. 60¢; 6. 70¢

Page 23
1. 12; 2. 15; 3. 17; 4. 11; 5. 14;
6. 16; 7. 16; 8. 14; 9. 15; 10. 14;
11. 7; 12. 10

Page 24
1. 5 cows; 2. 8 goats; 3. horses;
4. sheep; 5. hens and cows

Page 25
1. 3 inches; 2. 2 inches; 3. 5 inches;
4. 3 inches

Page 26
1. 14; 2. 15; 3. 9; 4. 4; 5. 10;
6. 6; 7. 2; 8. 7; In a snowbank

Page 27
The dots should be connected to form a telescope.

Page 28
1. 7; 2. 4; 3. 1; 4. 2; 5. 3; 6. 5;
7. 8; 8. 6; 9. 3; 10. 8; 11. 8; 12. 9;
In a "neigh-borhood"

Page 29
1. 11¢; 2. 10¢; 3. 3¢; 4. 7¢; 5. 16¢;
6. 11¢

Page 30
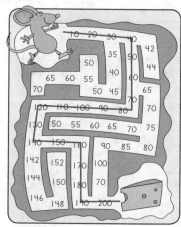

Page 31
Check that these problems are circled: 2. 4 + 5 = 9;
3. 3 + 3 = 6; 4. 6 + 1 = 7;
5. 8 − 2 = 6; 6. 8 − 1 = 7;
7. 2 + 3 = 5; 8. 8 − 5 = 3;
A goldfish

Page 32
Check that the letters in 1, 2, 4, 6, 7, 9, and 11 are circled; Trouble

Page 33
Check that the correct numbers are colored; 1. 14, 18; 2. 24, 28; 3. 2, 6, 8; 4. 30, 36, 38; 5. 20, 22, 24; 6. 34, 38

Page 34
Check that the directions are correctly followed.

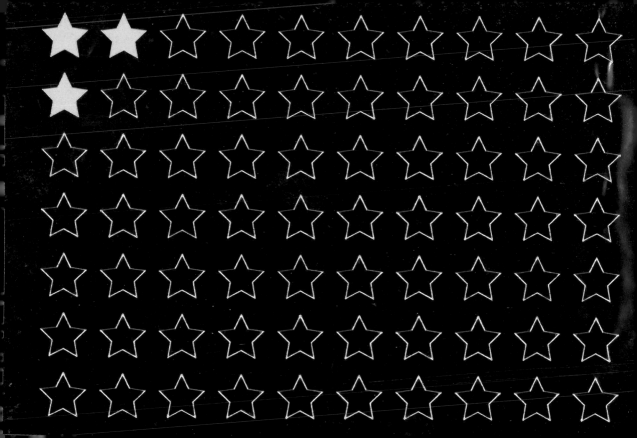

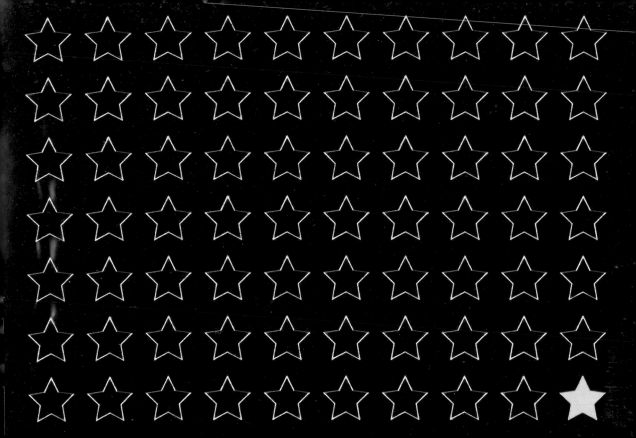

Page 35
Check that these numbers are written in each problem: 1. 2; 2. 6; 3. 3; 4. 7; 5. 4; 6. 5; A "carpet"

Page 36

Page 37
1. 5; 2. 9; 3. 8; 4. 10; 5. 7; 6. 6; 7. 7; 8. 9; 9. 10; 10. 8; 11. 7; 12. 9; 13. 7; 14. 10; 15. 6; 16. 10

Page 38
1. Friday; 2. Wednesday; 3. Monday; 4. Monday

Page 39
1. 8; 2. 7; 3. 9; 4. 9; 5. 6; 6. 9; 7. 4; 8. 8; 9. 6; 10. 4; 11. 6; 12. 4

Page 40
1. 12 – 1 = 11 children
2. 4 + 4 = 8 miles
3. 3 + 3 = 6 scoops of food
4. 8 + 5 = 13 years old
5. 12 – 8 = 4 birds
6. 10 – 9 = 1 truck

Page 41

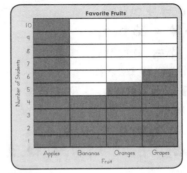

Page 42
1. purple; 2. 6; 3. blue; 4. red and yellow

Page 43
1. 90¢ – 70¢ = 20¢
2. 10¢ + 60¢ = 70¢
3. 60¢ – 50¢ = 10¢
4. 90¢ – 50¢ = 40¢
5. 30¢ + 10¢ = 40¢
6. 50¢ + 30¢ = 80¢

Page 44
Check that these numbers are written in each problem: 1. 11; 2. 12; 3. 5; 4. 8; 5. 6; 6. 7; Swimming trunks

Page 45
Answers will vary but one space in each shape should be colored.

Page 46

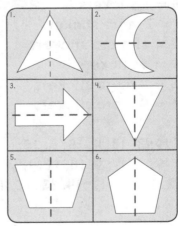

Page 47
1. 10 – 6 = 4 cats;
2. 14 + 4 = 18 birds;
3. 15 + 3 = 18 ants;
4. 18 – 7 = 11 bees;
5. 8 – 3 = 5 fish; 6. 3 + 1 = 4 dogs

Page 48
1. 4; 2. 9; 3. 9; 4. 9; 5. 9; 6. 4;
7. 8; 8. 8; 9. 8; 10. 4; 11. 6; 12. 2

Page 49
1. blue; 2. yellow; 3. green;
4. blue

Page 50

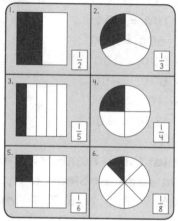

Page 51
1. 51¢; 2. 60¢; 3. 12¢; 4. 45¢;
5. 1¢

Page 52
1. 10 – 5 = 5 stickers
2. 9 – 2 = 7 more stickers
3. 18 – 7 = 11 more stickers
4. 12 – 9 = 3 stickers
5. 12 – 8 = 4 more stickers
6. 10 – 6 = 4 more stickers

Page 53
1. 19; 2. 19; 3. 18; 4. 15; 5. 15;
6. 17; 7. 19; 8. 17; 9. 18; 10. 17;
11. 12; 12. 18; 13. 17; 14. 13; 15. 18

Page 54
1. 10 o'clock; 2. 12 o'clock;
3. half past 9:00; 4. half past 3:00;
5. half past 10:00; 6. 7 o'clock

Page 55
1. 6 + 2 = 8 crayons
2. 8 + 7 = 15 pencils
3. 5 + 3 = 8 paper clips
4. 5 + 1 = 6 pens
5. 7 + 2 = 9 erasers
6. 3 + 3 = 6 markers

Page 56
1. Monday; 2. 3 + 5 = 8 toads and
frogs; 3. 5 – 3 = 2 frogs;
4. 7 + 5 + 4 = 16 frogs; 5. Tuesday;
6. Monday

Page 57
1. 3:00; 2. 12:00; 3. 4:00; 4. 7:00;
5. 11:00; 6. 9:00

Page 58
1. no; 2. no; 3. yes; 4. yes

Page 59

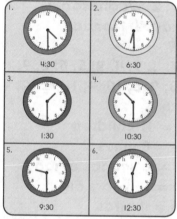

Page 60
1. 6; 2. 2; 3. 8; 4. 8; 5. 5; 6. 5;
7. 5; 8. 3; 9. 7; 10. 8; 11. 2; 12. 6

Circle the fact that does not belong in each fact family. To solve the riddle, write the circled letters in order on the lines. The first one has been done for you.

1. 4 – 3 = 1   C
   4 – 1 = 3   F
   (5 – 1 = 4) G
   1 + 3 = 4   E
   3 + 1 = 4   B

2. 5 – 4 = 1   U
   4 + 5 = 9   O
   5 – 1 = 4   E
   1 + 4 = 5   A
   4 + 1 = 5   I

3. 5 – 3 = 2   S
   5 – 2 = 3   M
   3 + 3 = 6   L
   2 + 3 = 5   N
   3 + 2 = 5   R

4. 6 – 5 = 1   C
   1 + 5 = 6   F
   6 + 1 = 7   D
   6 – 1 = 5   E
   5 + 1 = 6   G

5. 8 – 2 = 6   F
   6 – 4 = 2   J
   6 – 2 = 4   K
   2 + 4 = 6   L
   4 + 2 = 6   N

6. 7 – 6 = 1   O
   7 – 1 = 6   L
   6 + 1 = 7   K
   1 + 6 = 7   J
   8 – 1 = 7   I

7. 7 – 5 = 2   L
   2 + 5 = 7   R
   7 – 2 = 5   T
   2 + 3 = 5   S
   5 + 2 = 7   N

8. 7 – 4 = 3   T
   7 – 3 = 4   N
   8 – 5 = 3   H
   3 + 4 = 7   R
   4 + 3 = 7   S

What is the most expensive fish?

A G ___ ___ ___ ___ ___ ___ ___ ___

   CD-104359

Circle the letter beside each shape that is divided into equal halves. To solve the riddle, write the circled letters in order on the lines.

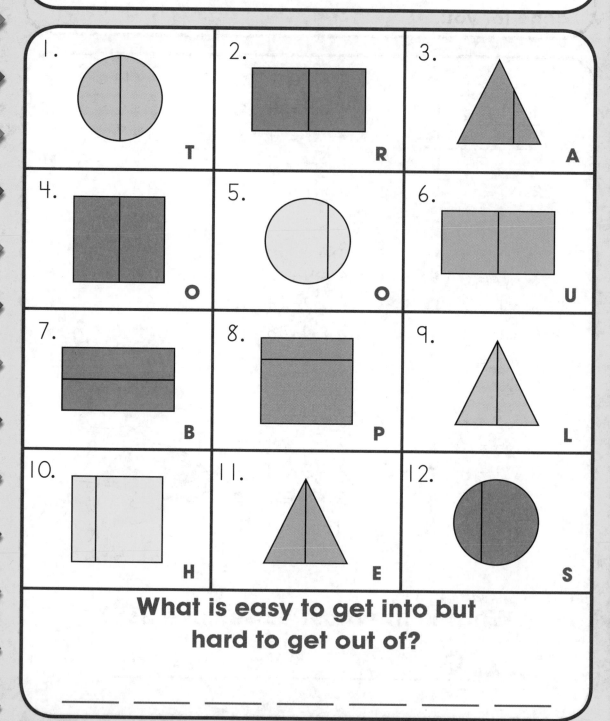

1. T

2. R

3. A

4. O

5. O

6. U

7. B

8. P

9. L

10. H

11. E

12. S

What is easy to get into but hard to get out of?

_____ _____ _____ _____ _____ _____

CD-104359

Start at 2. Count by 2s. Color each space you count.

1	2	3	4	5	6	7	8	9	10
11	12	13	14	15	16	17	18	19	20
21	22	23	24	25	26	27	28	29	30
31	32	33	34	35	36	37	38	39	40

Count by 2s. Write the missing numbers.

1.

10, 12, _____, 16, _____

2.

20, 22, _____, 26, _____

3.

_____, 4, _____, _____, 10

4.

_____, 32, 34, _____, _____

5.

18, _____, _____, _____, 26

6.

32, _____, 36, _____, 40

Follow the directions.

Count by 2s to 50.

__2__, _____, _____, _____, _____, _____, _____,

_____, _____, _____, _____, _____, _____, _____,

_____, _____, _____, _____, _____, _____, _____,

_____, _____, _____, _____

Count by 10s to 100.

__10__, _____, _____, _____, _____, _____, _____,

_____, _____, _____

Count by 5s to 100.

__5__, _____, _____, _____, _____, _____, _____,

_____, _____, _____, _____, _____, _____, _____,

_____, _____, _____, _____, _____, _____

CD-104359

Write the missing number from each fact family.
Match the answers to the numbers below. To solve
the riddle, write the correct letters on the lines.

1. **A**

_____ + 7 = 9

9 – 7 = _____

7 + _____ = 9

9 – _____ = 7

2. **C**

8 – 2 = _____

8 – _____ = 2

2 + _____ = 8

_____ + 2 = 8

3. **T**

_____ + 6 = 9

9 – 6 = _____

6 + _____ = 9

9 – _____ = 6

4. **E**

8 – 1 = _____

1 + _____ = 8

8 – _____ = 1

_____ + 1 = 8

5. **P**

9 – _____ = 5

5 + _____ = 9

_____ + 5 = 9

9 – 5 = _____

6. **R**

8 – _____ = 3

_____ + 3 = 8

3 + _____ = 8

8 – 3 = _____

What kind of pet is always on the floor?

A " ___ ___ ___ ___ ___ ___ "
    6   2   5   4   7   3

Fill in the missing times so that each set of clocks shows the same time. Write the time on the line. The first one has been done for you.

1.

___five___ o'clock

2.

eight o'clock

3.

_____ o'clock

4.

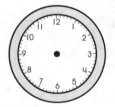 

_____ o'clock

5.

_____ o'clock

6.

two o'clock

Solve each problem.

1. $2 + 0 + 3 =$ _____

2. $5 + 3 + 1 =$ _____

3. $6 + 2 + 0 =$ _____

4. $6 + 3 + 1 =$ _____

5. $6 + 0 + 1 =$ _____

6. $4 + 0 + 2 =$ _____

7. $3 + 0 + 4 =$ _____

8. $3 + 3 + 3 =$ _____

9. $2 + 2 + 6 =$ _____

10. $7 + 0 + 1 =$ _____

11. $2 + 3 + 2 =$ _____

12. $8 + 0 + 1 =$ _____

13. $5 + 1 + 1 =$ _____

14. $3 + 6 + 1 =$ _____

15. $2 + 2 + 2 =$ _____

16. $7 + 2 + 1 =$ _____

Use the calendar to answer each question.

February

Sunday	Monday	Tuesday	Wednesday	Thursday	Friday	Saturday
		1	2	3	4	5
6	7	8	9	10	11	12
13	14	15	16	17	18	19
20	21	22	23	24	25	26
27	28					

1. What day of the week is February 11?

_____

2. What day of the week is February 2?

_____

3. What day of the week is the last day of February?

_____

4. What day of the week is February 14?

_____

CD-104359

Write the missing addend in each problem.

1.
$$\begin{array}{r} 4 \\ + \boxed{} \\ \hline 12 \end{array}$$

2.
$$\begin{array}{r} 6 \\ + \boxed{} \\ \hline 13 \end{array}$$

3.
$$\begin{array}{r} 9 \\ + \boxed{} \\ \hline 18 \end{array}$$

4.
$$\begin{array}{r} 4 \\ + \boxed{} \\ \hline 13 \end{array}$$

5.
$$\begin{array}{r} 4 \\ + \boxed{} \\ \hline 10 \end{array}$$

6.
$$\begin{array}{r} 7 \\ + \boxed{} \\ \hline 16 \end{array}$$

7.
$$\begin{array}{r} 7 \\ + \boxed{} \\ \hline 11 \end{array}$$

8.
$$\begin{array}{r} 6 \\ + \boxed{} \\ \hline 14 \end{array}$$

9.
$$\begin{array}{r} 8 \\ + \boxed{} \\ \hline 14 \end{array}$$

10.
$$\begin{array}{r} 8 \\ + \boxed{} \\ \hline 12 \end{array}$$

11.
$$\begin{array}{r} 5 \\ + \boxed{} \\ \hline 11 \end{array}$$

12.
$$\begin{array}{r} 9 \\ + \boxed{} \\ \hline 13 \end{array}$$

Solve each word problem.

1. Twelve children are playing on the swings. One child leaves. How many children are still playing on the swings?

   _____

2. A family travels 4 miles to the beach. Then, the family travels home. How many total miles did the family travel?

   _____

3. The farmer's horse eats 3 scoops of food each day. How many scoops of food will the horse eat in 2 days?

   _____

4. Ella is 8 years old. Her brother is 5 years older than her. How old is Ella's brother?

   _____

5. Ivan sees 12 birds. Eight birds are yellow. How many birds are not yellow?

   _____

6. Shawn has 10 toy trucks. Nine of the trucks are red. How many trucks are not red?

   _____

Use the data to complete the bar graph.

Fruit	Number of Students
Apples	卌 卌
Bananas	IIII
Oranges	卌
Grapes	卌 I

Favorite Fruits

Number of Students

	Apples	Bananas	Oranges	Grapes
10				
9				
8				
7				
6				
5				
4				
3				
2				
1				

Fruit

Use the graph to answer each question.

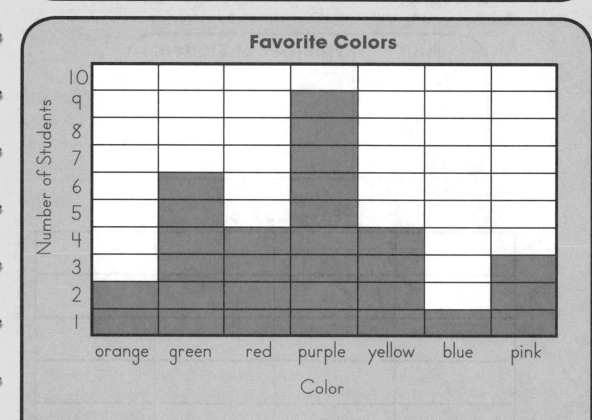

Favorite Colors

1. What color did the greatest number of students like?

_____

2. How many students liked green the most? _____

3. What color did the least number of students like?

_____

4. Which two colors had the same number of votes?

_____

_____

Solve each word problem.

1. Carrie has 90¢. She buys a pencil for 70¢. How much money does she have left?

_____

2. Pablo buys a pretzel for 10¢ and a banana for 60¢. How much money does he spend in all?

_____

3. Tisha has 60¢. She buys a muffin for 50¢. How much money does she have left?

_____

4. Trevor has 90¢. He buys milk for 50¢. How much money does he have left?

_____

5. Julio buys an eraser for 30¢ and a bookmark for 10¢. How much money does he spend in all?

_____

6. Hannah buys a muffin for 50¢ and juice for 30¢. How much money does she spend in all?

_____

Write the missing number from each fact family. Match the answers to the numbers below. To solve the riddle, write the correct letters on the lines.

1. **S**

$10 + 1 =$ _____

_____ $- 1 = 10$

$1 + 10 =$ _____

_____ $- 10 = 1$

2. **T**

_____ $- 10 = 2$

$2 + 10 =$ _____

$10 + 2 =$ _____

_____ $- 2 = 10$

3. **U**

$6 +$ _____ $= 11$

$11 - 6 =$ _____

$11 -$ _____ $= 6$

_____ $+ 6 = 11$

4. **N**

$3 +$ _____ $= 11$

$11 - 3 =$ _____

_____ $+ 3 = 11$

$11 -$ _____ $= 3$

5. **R**

$10 -$ _____ $= 4$

$4 +$ _____ $= 10$

_____ $+ 4 = 10$

$10 - 4 =$ _____

6. **K**

$10 -$ _____ $= 3$

_____ $+ 3 = 10$

$3 +$ _____ $= 10$

$10 - 3 =$ _____

What do you get when you cross an elephant and a fish?

Swimming

___ ___ ___ ___ ___ ___
12   6   5   8   7   11

CD-104359

Color $\frac{1}{4}$ of each shape.

1.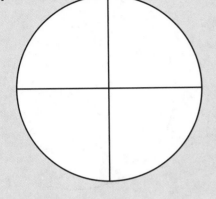

2.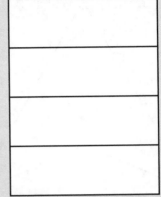

3.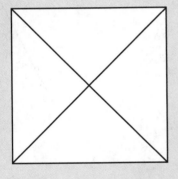

4.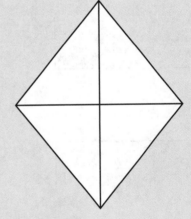

5.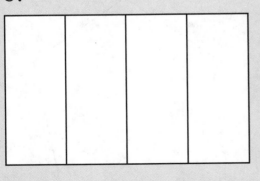

6.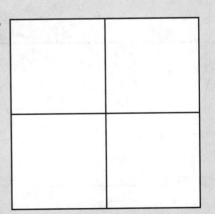

CD-104359 **45**

Draw a line of symmetry on each figure so that each half is the same. The first one has been done for you.

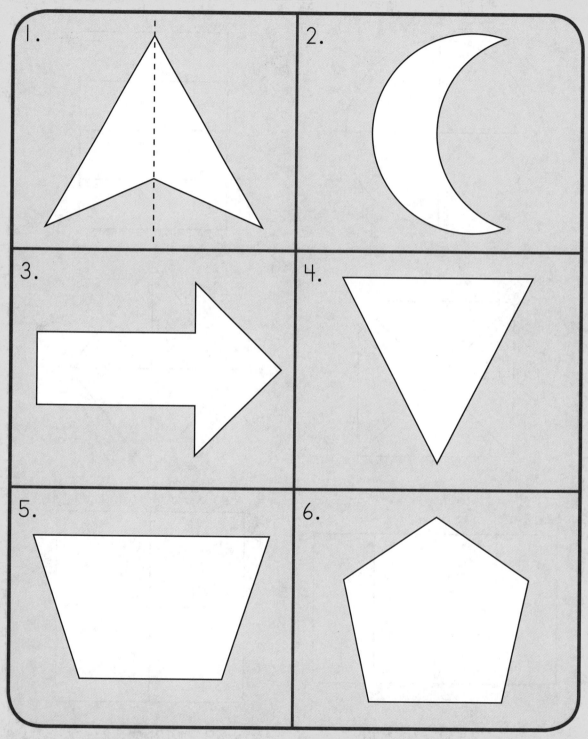

1.

2.

3.

4.

5.

6.

CD-104359

© Carson-Dellosa

Solve each word problem.

1. There are 10 cats sitting on a fence. Six cats leave. How many cats are left sitting on the fence?

   _____

2. Grace sees 14 birds at a bird feeder. Four more birds fly over to eat. How many birds are at the bird feeder in all?

   _____

3. Reid sees 15 black ants and 3 red ants. How many ants does Reid see in all?

   _____

4. There are 18 bees at a hive. Seven bees fly away. How many bees are left at the hive?

   _____

5. Cayce has 8 pet fish. Three fish are blue. How many fish are not blue?

   _____

6. Juan has 3 dogs. His sister gives him 1 dog. How many dogs does Juan have in all?

   _____

Write the missing addend in each problem.

1.
$$\begin{array}{r} 8 \\ + \boxed{} \\ \hline 12 \end{array}$$

2.
$$\begin{array}{r} 5 \\ + \boxed{} \\ \hline 14 \end{array}$$

3.
$$\begin{array}{r} 9 \\ + \boxed{} \\ \hline 18 \end{array}$$

4.
$$\begin{array}{r} 4 \\ + \boxed{} \\ \hline 13 \end{array}$$

5.
$$\begin{array}{r} 8 \\ + \boxed{} \\ \hline 17 \end{array}$$

6.
$$\begin{array}{r} 7 \\ + \boxed{} \\ \hline 11 \end{array}$$

7.
$$\begin{array}{r} 6 \\ + \boxed{} \\ \hline 14 \end{array}$$

8.
$$\begin{array}{r} 8 \\ + \boxed{} \\ \hline 16 \end{array}$$

9.
$$\begin{array}{r} 3 \\ + \boxed{} \\ \hline 11 \end{array}$$

10.
$$\begin{array}{r} 9 \\ + \boxed{} \\ \hline 13 \end{array}$$

11.
$$\begin{array}{r} 9 \\ + \boxed{} \\ \hline 15 \end{array}$$

12.
$$\begin{array}{r} 10 \\ + \boxed{} \\ \hline 12 \end{array}$$

CD-104359

Use the spinner to answer each question.

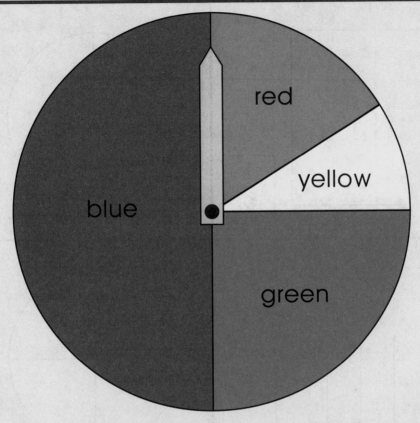

1. Which color will the spinner probably land on most often?

   _____

2. Which color will the spinner probably land on least often?

   _____

3. Will the spinner be more likely to land on yellow or green?

   _____

4. Will the spinner be more likely to land on red or blue?

   _____

CD-104359   **49**

Color each shape to show the fraction.

1.
$\dfrac{1}{2}$

2.
$\dfrac{1}{3}$

3.
$\dfrac{1}{5}$

4.
$\dfrac{1}{4}$

5.
$\dfrac{1}{6}$

6.
$\dfrac{1}{8}$

Calculate the change in each row. Circle the answer.

1. 25¢ 50¢ 1¢ 1¢ − 25¢ 1¢ = 51¢   50¢   26¢

2. 50¢ 25¢ 10¢ − 25¢ = 60¢   25¢   85¢

3. 25¢ 1¢ 1¢ 1¢ 10¢ − 25¢ 1¢ = 26¢   38¢   12¢

4. 50¢ 25¢ 10¢ 10¢ − 50¢ = 50¢   45¢   95¢

5. 25¢ 1¢ − 25¢ = 5¢   25¢   1¢

Solve each word problem.

1. Kate earned 10 airplane stickers and 5 animal stickers. How many more airplane stickers than animal stickers did she earn?

_____

2. Charlie earned 9 truck stickers and 2 dinosaur stickers. How many more truck stickers than dinosaur stickers did he earn?

_____

3. Wayne earned 18 sports stickers and 7 airplane stickers. How many more sports stickers than airplane stickers did he earn?

_____

4. Lin had 12 dog stickers. She gave 9 of them away. How many dog stickers did Lin have left?

_____

5. Kori earned 12 plant stickers and 8 truck stickers. How many more plant stickers than truck stickers did he earn?

_____

6. Rosa earned 10 animal stickers and 6 dinosaur stickers. How many more animal stickers than dinosaur stickers did she earn?

_____

CD-104359

Solve each problem.

1. $\begin{array}{r} 15 \\ + 4 \\ \hline \end{array}$

2. $\begin{array}{r} 12 \\ + 7 \\ \hline \end{array}$

3. $\begin{array}{r} 17 \\ + 1 \\ \hline \end{array}$

4. $\begin{array}{r} 12 \\ + 3 \\ \hline \end{array}$

5. $\begin{array}{r} 10 \\ + 5 \\ \hline \end{array}$

6. $\begin{array}{r} 15 \\ + 2 \\ \hline \end{array}$

7. $\begin{array}{r} 11 \\ + 8 \\ \hline \end{array}$

8. $\begin{array}{r} 11 \\ + 6 \\ \hline \end{array}$

9. $\begin{array}{r} 13 \\ + 5 \\ \hline \end{array}$

10. $\begin{array}{r} 10 \\ + 7 \\ \hline \end{array}$

11. $\begin{array}{r} 10 \\ + 2 \\ \hline \end{array}$

12. $\begin{array}{r} 16 \\ + 2 \\ \hline \end{array}$

13. $\begin{array}{r} 14 \\ + 3 \\ \hline \end{array}$

14. $\begin{array}{r} 12 \\ + 1 \\ \hline \end{array}$

15. $\begin{array}{r} 14 \\ + 4 \\ \hline \end{array}$

Circle the correct time below each clock.

1.

A. 10 o'clock

B. 9 o'clock

C. 11 o'clock

2.

A. 11 o'clock

B. 12 o'clock

C. 1 o'clock

3.

A. half past 9:00

B. half past 8:00

C. half past 10:00

4.

A. half past 2:00

B. half past 3:00

C. half past 4:00

5.

A. half past 6:00

B. half past 9:00

C. half past 10:00

6.

A. 7 o'clock

B. 8 o'clock

C. 9 o'clock

Solve each word problem.

1. Jayla counted 6 red crayons and 2 blue crayons. How many crayons did Jayla count in all?

   _____

2. Lauren had 8 yellow pencils and 7 red pencils. How many pencils did she have in all?

   _____

3. Clint found 5 green paper clips and 3 brown paper clips. How many paper clips did he find in all?

   _____

4. Kevin counted 5 black pens and 1 blue pen. How many pens did he count in all?

   _____

5. Paula had 7 pink erasers and 2 green erasers. How many erasers did she have in all?

   _____

6. Brett borrowed 3 blue markers and 3 green markers. How many markers did he borrow in all?

   _____

Use the table to answer each question.

Frogs and Toads in Randy's Pond

	Monday	Tuesday	Wednesday
Frogs	7	5	4
Toads	6	3	8

1. On which day were the most frogs in the pond?

   _____

2. How many toads and frogs were in the pond on Tuesday?

   _____ + _____ = _____

3. How many more frogs than toads were in the pond
   on Tuesday? _____ – _____ = _____

4. How many frogs were in the pond all three days?

   _____ + _____ + _____ = _____

5. On which day were the fewest toads in the pond?

   _____

6. On which day were there 13 toads and frogs in the pond
   altogether? _____